My Little FUN FAX

Finding Out

Baby Animals

Written by Nicola Baxter
Illustrated by Diana Bowles

© Henderson Publishing Limited 1993

Henderson
Woodbridge, England *Publishing*

Baby animals love to play

They play chasing games ....

hide and seek ....

running ....

jumping ....

creeping ever
so quietly
and .....

pouncing!

Small families

Some animals have only one or two babies at a time.

Large families

Some animals have lots of babies!

Hungry babies

Some babies are hungry all the time!
This mother pig can feed nearly all her piglets at once.

Don't worry little piglet,
your turn next.

Owls go hunting at night to find food for their babies.
Which owlet is going to get the mouse this time?

Safe and sound babies

Baby animals have to learn to stay safe, just like you. A baby deer's spotted coat makes her hard to see under the trees.

Baby woodpeckers stay safe in their nest until they learn to fly.

Baby badgers stay safe in their setts underground.

Babies are carried

Some baby animals can't walk when they are born. They have to be carried.

A mother kangaroo has a pouch to carry her baby in. It is a special furry pocket. A baby kangaroo is called a joey.

A baby monkey holds on tight to his mother's fur as she swings through the trees.

The tiny baby koala lives snuggly in its mother's pouch for five long months.

A tigress carries her tiger cub gently in her mouth.

Come on cubs, time for your nap.

Mother crocodile lays a great pile of eggs. She guards them until the babies hatch.

She carries her babies in her mouth down to the river.

Babies that hatch

A hen makes her nest and starts to lay her eggs.

And she sits ...... until one day she hears a tiny sound.

Peck, peck! Something is happening inside the eggs.

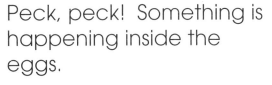

When they dry out, there is a very fluffy little chick.

Out pops a little chick. His feathers are wet.

Daddy ostrich helps to keep the eggs warm.

A baby ostrich hatches from this huge egg.

Same as mum and dad

Some animal babies look quite like their mother and father. Only they are much, much smaller!

This calf is having fun squirting water.

This baby hippopotamus looks just like his mother. He acts like her too and loves to swim and play in the river.

What a big mouth
this baby hippo has.

Different to mum and dad

Other babies don't look like their mother and father when they are tiny.

Baby swans are called cygnets.
At first, the cygnets are grey and fluffy.

But as they grow older, the cygnets' feathers become white and smooth. Soon they are graceful grown-up swans.

Who would have thought such a pretty walrus pup could grow to look like Dad?

This pup is having fun sliding on the ice.

Babies that never need their parents

A frog lays lots of eggs in the pond and she leaves them to grow on their own.

The little black part in the middle of the egg starts to grow into a tadpole.

First the tadpoles grow back legs and then front legs.

At last they become little frogs and swim up to jump in the sun!

Sea Turtles lay lots of eggs in the sand. She leaves the eggs to hatch on their own.

When the babies hatch, they have to find their way to the sea all by themselves.

Feeding from mummy

When some animals are very young, they take food from mummy.

The calf drinks milk from its mother. When it grows up, it will eat the grass just like its parents.

In the spring, the kids love to chase and playfully butt each other. They also love to drink the milk from their mother.

Lost babies

These baby animals have lost their mothers. Which mothers do these babies belong to?

Babies

Mothers